Five One-Act Plays

DONN BYRNE

Level 3

Series Editors: Andy Hopkins and Jocelyn Potter

Pearson Education Limited
Edinburgh Gate, Harlow,
Essex CM20 2JE, England
and Associated Companies throughout the world.

ISBN: 978-1-4058-8182-1

First published 2000
This edition first published 2008

7

Text copyright © Donn Byrne 2008
Illustrations by Chris Long

Typeset by Graphicraft Ltd, Hong Kong
Set in 11/14pt Bembo
Printed in China
SWTC/07

Published by Pearson Education Ltd

For a complete list of the titles available in the Pearson English Readers series, please visit
www.pearsonenglishreaders.com.
Alternatively, write to your local Pearson Education office or to Pearson English Readers
Marketing Department, Pearson Education, Edinburgh Gate, Harlow, Essex CM20 2JE, England.

Contents

Introduction

JOHN	*Look, there's her book. In the sea!*
MARY	*And her umbrella!*
MR BROWN	*But where's her chair? I can't see it.*
MRS BROWN	*It's at the bottom of the sea. With Granny on it. I've killed her!*

Has Mrs Brown killed Granny? Why doesn't Mrs Stone want to let her room to the old man? Why does Mrs Hill want to leave her husband? Who are the men from London who come for the Professor's invention? And what is little Johnny trying to say?

Here are five plays about ordinary people and the unusual, often funny, things that happen to them.

In 'Listen to the Boy!' a small boy in a shop wants to say something important, but the adults aren't listening to him. This often happens but is it a mistake? In 'The Right Person' there is a young man and an old man. Which of the two men is cleverer? We meet Granny in 'An Afternoon on the Beach'. She's old and she can't walk very fast, but she isn't stupid. Her family – well, how clever are they? Mr Hill, in 'A Bad Dream', doesn't think that his cook is very good at her job. He thinks she should find a new job. But is he good at *his* job? 'The Professor' is about an old man. He often loses his glasses. Sometimes he can't find his watch. But he has an important invention that people want to steal. Will he be cleverer than them, or will he lose his invention too?

You will find the answers to all these questions when you read these plays. And when you have finished reading, you can act out the plays with your friends.

Donn Byrne worked for the British Council for many years in Europe, South America and India. He has written many books for teachers and students of English. He now writes fiction from his home in Scotland.

Listen to the Boy!

CHARACTERS

MR SMITH
MISS WHITE
MRS BALL
MRS WOOD
JOHNNY BELL

(MR SMITH is in his greengrocer's shop. Three women are waiting.)

MR SMITH	Yes? Who's next, please?
MISS WHITE	I think you're next, Mrs Ball. You were here before me, weren't you?
MRS BALL	Oh, was I? Thank you.
MR SMITH	What can I do for you, madam? Do you need any fruit?
MRS BALL	Yes, please. I'd like . . .

(A small boy runs into the shop. He pushes in front of the three women.)

JOHNNY	Please, Mr Smith . . .
MR SMITH	One minute, young man! I'm talking to this lady. And these two ladies are waiting. *(He turns to MRS BALL again.)* Yes, madam. What were you saying?
JOHNNY	But, sir!
MRS BALL	Be quiet! I want two kilos of potatoes, Mr Smith.
MR SMITH	Two kilos of potatoes. Of course. I have some good ones here. *(He points to some potatoes.)* Eighty pence a kilo. Are these all right?
MRS BALL	Yes, I'll take those.

1

MRS WOOD	*(Looking at* JOHNNY*)* Children today! They're so rude!
MISS WHITE	They can't wait! They always want to be first!
MRS WOOD	How old are you?
JOHNNY	Nine, er . . .
MRS WOOD	Only nine! And you pushed in front of this lady.
JOHNNY	I had to. I wanted . . .
MISS WHITE	*(Before he can finish)* Young people must learn to wait. You can't push in front of people. You're not the only customer in the shop, you know.
MRS BALL	Did your mother send you?
JOHNNY	No. I wanted . . .
MRS WOOD	*(Quickly)* Ah, you wanted something! You couldn't wait, could you? What's your name?
JOHNNY	Johnny Bell.
MISS WHITE	You live in Church Street, don't you? I've seen you there.
JOHNNY	Yes, that's right.
MISS WHITE	I'll speak to your mother about you.
JOHNNY	But I only wanted . . .
MR SMITH	That's enough, young man. We don't want to hear. *(He turns to* MRS BALL.*)* Here you are, Mrs Ball. Two kilos of potatoes. Is that everything? That'll be one pound sixty, please. Thank you.

*(*MRS BALL *gives* MR SMITH *the money. She takes her potatoes and leaves.)*

2

MR SMITH   Next, please.

JOHNNY   I'm sorry but . . . *(Nobody listens to him.)*

MISS WHITE   I want some apples, please. One kilo.

MR SMITH   What about these? *(He points to some apples behind him.)*
They're only seventy pence a kilo.

MISS WHITE   No, they're too green. Are there any sweeter ones?

MR SMITH   Yes, madam. I've got some good ones, but they're still
in my car. Seventy-five pence a kilo.

MISS WHITE   Can I see them?

MR SMITH   I'll go and get them.

(MR SMITH goes out. A minute later he runs in again.)

MR SMITH   *(Shouting)* They're not there! There was a box of
apples in my car and now it's gone. The car's empty.

JOHNNY   I saw two men near your car, Mr Smith. They opened
the door and took out a box of apples.

MR SMITH   My apples! I've lost a big box of apples. *(He turns to
JOHNNY and shouts in an angry voice.)* Why didn't you
tell me?

JOHNNY   I tried to tell you, sir, but nobody listened to me!

The Right Person

CHARACTERS
MRS STONE
MR STONE
YOUNG MAN
OLD MAN

(An upstairs room in the Stones' house. MRS STONE wants to let the room. She is standing next to her husband.)

MRS STONE	Well, the room's ready. I've worked very hard. I hope I can let it. What do you think?
MR STONE	Somebody will like it, I'm sure. People need rooms.
MRS STONE	But you don't seem to like it very much. What's wrong with it? Tell me. It's big enough, isn't it?
MR STONE	Yes, it's not a small room.
MRS STONE	And it's clean, too.
MR STONE	Yes, it's clean.
MRS STONE	What's wrong, then? Is it the furniture? Don't you like it?

MR STONE	It's a little heavy, I think. And old, too.
MRS STONE	But it's very *good* furniture. It belonged to my mother.
MR STONE	That's the problem. It's good, but it's too old. People today prefer *modern* furniture.
MRS STONE	That's not true. People go to the shops and buy old furniture like this.
MR STONE	Yes, but those people won't come here. They have their own houses. But why do you want to let this room? It isn't necessary. We've got enough money, haven't we?
MRS STONE	Yes, of course we've got enough money. That isn't the reason.
MR STONE	What *is* the reason, then?
MRS STONE	I want something to do. I get bored at home all day.
MR STONE	Well, I hope a nice person takes the room. A quiet person. I don't want a lot of noise in the house.
MRS STONE	I'll let it to the right person. A nice young man. Two people are coming this morning. They phoned last night. They'll be here soon.

(MRS STONE *crosses to the window. Her husband follows. They both look out of the window.*)

MRS STONE	There's a nice view from the room, isn't there? You can see a long way.
MR STONE	Yes, it's a nice view. But people won't take the room for the view. *(He points out of the window.)* Look, a young man's coming to the house.
MRS STONE	*(Looking at her watch)* Yes, he's on time. I liked his voice on the phone. He spoke very nicely. I think he comes from a good family.

MR STONE   Well, he won't like this room!

*(The doorbell rings. MRS STONE goes downstairs to open the door.
MR STONE walks round the room and then stops in front of the fireplace.)*

MR STONE   *(Talking to himself)* Hmm, this wall doesn't look very strong.

(He pushes the wall very hard and a piece falls out.)

MR STONE   Oh no! What have I done now? I hope nobody sees the hole.

(MRS STONE returns, followed by the young man.)

MRS STONE   Well, this is the room. Do you like it?

YOUNG MAN   Hmm. I was looking for a bigger room. And where did you find this furniture? It's very old, isn't it?

MRS STONE   *(Coldly)* It belonged to my mother. She always paid a lot of money for her furniture.

YOUNG MAN   Ah, it belonged to your mother. Now I understand. *(He crosses the room and sits down on the bed.)* This bed's too hard. I like a soft one. I can't sleep on a bed like this.

MRS STONE   Oh, we can change the bed. We'll get a soft one for you.

(The YOUNG MAN gets up and walks to the window.)

MR STONE   It's a nice view, isn't it? Do you like it? You can see a long way.

YOUNG MAN   Can you? Views don't interest me. I'm out all day. You can't look at views when it's dark.

(The YOUNG MAN walks across the room. He stops in front of the fireplace. He sees the hole in the wall.)

YOUNG MAN   Look at this hole. The wall's falling down!

MRS STONE	*(Seeing the hole for the first time)* I've never seen that hole before. *(She turns to her husband.)* When did *that* happen?
MR STONE	A few minutes ago. I only touched it and a piece fell out. It's all right. I can repair it.

(MRS STONE gives her husband an angry look.)

YOUNG MAN	It's an old house. These things happen, of course.
MRS STONE	My husband can soon repair it.
YOUNG MAN	How much do you want for the room?
MRS STONE	Seventy pounds a week.
YOUNG MAN	Seventy pounds! That's a lot of money for this room.
MRS STONE	With breakfast. I'll give you a good breakfast.
YOUNG MAN	I don't eat breakfast. I get up late, so I don't have time.
MRS STONE	Then you can have the room for sixty pounds. And I'll wash your clothes for you.
YOUNG MAN	I'll think about it. I can't give you an answer now. *(He goes to the door.)* I'll phone you this afternoon. Is that all right?
MRS STONE	Yes, of course.
YOUNG MAN	Thank you. Goodbye.
MRS STONE	*(To her husband)* Can you go to the door with the young man, Harry?

(MR STONE goes out with the young man. After a short time he comes back.)

MRS STONE	Do you think he wants the room?
MR STONE	No, of course not. He didn't like it. He won't phone.

MRS STONE	I hope he takes it. I liked him.
MR STONE	*I* didn't!
MRS STONE	*(In an angry voice.)* And that hole over the fireplace! Why did you do that?
MR STONE	I told you, dear. I only touched the wall and a piece fell out.
MRS STONE	It isn't possible.

(The doorbell rings again. They cross to the window and look out.)

MR STONE	There's another man at the door.
MRS STONE	He looks quite old. I thought he was younger on the phone.
MR STONE	Shall I go and open the door?
MRS STONE	Can't we stay here? He doesn't know we're in. Perhaps he won't wait.

(The doorbell rings again.)

MR STONE	He knows we're in the house. Perhaps he saw the young man when he came out.
MRS STONE	What shall I say to him? I don't want to look after an old man. What will I do if he gets ill?
MR STONE	But he must see the room. Perhaps he's come a long way.
MRS STONE	All right, he can come in. But he can't have the room.

(MR STONE goes out. He comes back with the OLD MAN.)

OLD MAN	Good morning, Mrs Stone. My name's Arthur Dean. I phoned you about the room.
MRS STONE	Yes, I know. But I'm very sorry. Somebody's already taken the room.

OLD MAN	Already?
MRS STONE	Yes, I've let it. A young man came a short time ago and he's taken it.
OLD MAN	Oh, I met a young man near your house. Perhaps it was the same person. I stopped him in the street and asked him the way.
MR STONE	Yes, that was the young man. He left a few minutes ago.
OLD MAN	But he didn't like the room. He told me. *(He looks round the room.)* But *I* like it. I think it's very nice.
MRS STONE	We live a long way from the town. There aren't a lot of buses. Only one an hour.
OLD MAN	Oh, that doesn't matter. I don't work. When I go to town, I can walk. I enjoy a walk. And your house is very quiet. Not many houses are as quiet as this.
MRS STONE	It's quiet now. But my husband shouts a lot. And I like listening to loud music. We're very noisy people.
OLD MAN	Oh, that doesn't worry me. I was talking about the noise of cars and buses.
MRS STONE	The room's quite cold in winter.
OLD MAN	I won't notice. I've got a lot of warm clothes. *(He crosses to the window.)* There's a nice view from here. I like a room with a view.
MR STONE	Yes, it *is* nice, isn't it?
MRS STONE	It's nice now. But they're going to build new houses there. When that happens, there won't be a view.
OLD MAN	Perhaps they'll never build them. Who knows?
MR STONE	What about the furniture? Do you like that?

OLD MAN	Yes, very much. I like old furniture.
MRS STONE	I'm afraid the bed's very hard. Try it.
OLD MAN	That's not necessary. I like a hard bed. Yes, I like this room very much. I need a room like this. I hope it doesn't cost a lot.
MRS STONE	Seventy pounds a week.
OLD MAN	Seventy pounds. Well, that's fine. I was ready to pay more than that for a good room. Is that with breakfast?
MR STONE	Yes, with breakfast.
MRS STONE	Of course, the room isn't quite ready. Look at that wall. *(She points to the wall over the fireplace.)* We'll have to repair it. It will take time.
OLD MAN	Oh, that doesn't matter. It's only a small hole. I can put a picture over it.
MR STONE	We have some old pictures somewhere. Where are they, Mary?
MRS STONE	I put them in the garage. I didn't like them.
OLD MAN	We can cover the hole with one of those.
MR STONE	I'll go and get one or two. You can have a look at them. *(He goes out of the room.)*
MRS STONE	So you don't work, Mr Dean?
OLD MAN	That's right. I stopped work two years ago. But before that, I worked in a museum.
MRS STONE	That's interesting. What did you do there?
OLD MAN	I looked after the pictures. I know a lot about pictures. I'm writing a book about them. So I need a quiet room. Like a museum!

MRS STONE   Yes, of course.

(MR STONE comes back with the pictures. He has one big picture and two smaller ones.)

MRS STONE   Mr Dean worked in a museum, Harry. He knows a lot about pictures.

MR STONE   Well, he won't like these! They're very dirty.

OLD MAN   *(Looking at the pictures)* Well, this big one will cover the hole.

MR STONE   Do you like it?

OLD MAN   It's not a bad picture. I'll clean it for you. I know about these things. *(He picks up one of the smaller pictures.)* Well, this is a surprise!

MR STONE   What is it?

(The OLD MAN takes the picture to the window. He looks at it very carefully.)

OLD MAN   Is this really yours?

MR STONE   Yes, of course. All these pictures belonged to my wife's mother. Why? Is it a good picture?

OLD MAN   Yes, it is. It was painted by John Holland. Look, you can see his name here. In the corner of the picture.

MRS STONE   Who *was* he? I've never heard of him.

OLD MAN   He lived about a hundred years ago. People didn't like his pictures then, but they like them now–

MR STONE   Really? And is the picture worth much?

OLD MAN   Oh, yes. It's worth quite a lot of money – about £5,000.

MR STONE   £5,000! Did you hear that, Mary? And you put it in the garage!

MRS STONE	I don't know what to say.
MR STONE	And there are a lot more pictures in the garage.
OLD MAN	Well, I must look at all of them. *(To MRS STONE)* But perhaps you don't want to let the room now. You'll be rich when you sell the pictures.
MRS STONE	No, of course you must have the room. And I'll be able to buy new furniture with the money.
OLD MAN	No, please don't do that! Not for me. I like this old furniture. Don't change it. I'm sure I'll be very happy here.

An Afternoon on the Beach

SCENE 1

(JOHN and MARY BROWN have come to the beach with their parents and their grandmother. The old lady is walking between MR and MRS BROWN. They are holding her arms. JOHN and MARY are in front. They are looking for a place on the beach. JOHN is carrying a chair for GRANNY. MARY has two baskets.)

JOHN Look, there's a nice place. Near the cliffs. *(They go there.)*

MARY Yes, this is fine. *(They put down the chair and baskets. MARY calls to her parents.)* We've found a nice place near the cliffs. Be quick.

MRS BROWN We can't come quickly. You know your grandmother can't walk very fast. We can't leave her.

GRANNY I'm all right! I'm not a child, you know!

MR BROWN But these stones are dangerous. We don't want you to fall.

MRS BROWN You have to be careful at your age.

(A short time later, they reach the place near the cliffs.)

MR BROWN Yes, this will be all right. But don't leave the baskets there, Mary. Put them out of the sun.

(MARY moves the baskets.)

JOHN Shall I move Granny's chair, too?

MRS BROWN No, leave it in the sun, John. *(She points.)* Over there, away from the cliffs. The sun will be good for her.

GRANNY But I don't want to sit in the sun! I want to read and have a little sleep.

MRS BROWN Put the chair there, John. *(JOHN takes the chair and puts it in the sun.)* That's right. *(To GRANNY)* Come with me, dear.

MR BROWN	Yes, the sun will be good for you. We don't often have a warm day like this.

(They take GRANNY to the chair. She sits down.)

MRS BROWN	There! It's nice in the sun, isn't it?
GRANNY	No. I don't want to sit here. I told you. Can I have something to drink?
MRS BROWN	No, not yet. It's only three o'clock. We'll have tea at four.

(MR and MRS BROWN sit down near GRANNY'S chair.)

MARY	What are we going to do this afternoon? Are we going to stay here?
JOHN	Can we go in the sea?
MRS BROWN	No, John. The water's too cold.
JOHN	*(To his father)* Can we go to the cave? You promised to take us there.
MRS BROWN	We can go later. I'm tired. I want to have a rest.
JOHN	No, we must go now. The sea will come in soon. Then we won't be able to reach the cave.
MR BROWN	We *should* take them. I promised.
MRS BROWN	Where is the cave? Is it far?
MARY	It's about two kilometres from here.
MRS BROWN	*(To her husband)* You take them, dear. I'll stay here and look after Granny.
GRANNY	Don't stay here for me. I'm all right.
MARY	Oh, please come with us, Mum.
MRS BROWN	But we can't leave Granny alone here.
GRANNY	I *want* to be alone! I want to read and have a rest.

15

MRS BROWN	Are you sure, dear? I don't like to leave you.
GRANNY	Yes, I'm quite sure. If you stay, you'll talk. I want to have a rest.
MRS BROWN	All right then. *(She gets up. MR BROWN does the same.)* Here's your book. And your umbrella, too. Put the umbrella up if you feel too warm.

(MR BROWN and the children walk away.)

MARY	*(Calling to her mother.)* Are you coming, Mum?
MRS BROWN	Yes, I'm ready. *(She turns to GRANNY as they go.)* Goodbye, dear. We'll soon be back. Then we'll have a nice cup of tea.
GRANNY	Goodbye. Have a nice time. *(She opens her book and begins to read. Then she looks up.)* Good, they've gone at last! Now I'll move my chair out of the sun. *(She puts her book on the sand. She stands up and carries her chair to the cliffs. She puts it behind a big rock. Then she sits down.)* Ah, it's nice behind this rock. *Now* I can have a good rest. *(She closes her eyes and is soon asleep.)*

SCENE 2

(In the cave.)

MR BROWN	Well, here we are at last!
MRS BROWN	It's dark in here. I can't see a thing.
MR BROWN	Wait a minute. I've got a box of matches.

(MR BROWN lights a match.)

MR BROWN	How's that? Now you can see.
MRS BROWN	It's cold and wet in here. I don't like it.

MARY	But it's a famous cave, Mum.
MRS BROWN	Why, what happened here?
MARY	Smugglers came here, didn't they?
MR BROWN	Yes, that's right. It was a smugglers' cave.
JOHN	Did they live here? In this cave?
MARY	No, they didn't *live* here, John. They brought things from the ships and hid them here.

(The light goes out and the cave is dark again. MR BROWN lights another match.)

JOHN	I want to go to the back of the cave. Can I have the matches, Dad?
MRS BROWN	No, stay here, John. It's dangerous. The floor of the cave is still wet from the sea.
MARY	What did the smugglers do when the sea came in? Where did they put their things?
JOHN	There are some holes in the walls. They're higher than the water. Perhaps the smugglers put their things there. Give me the matches, Dad, and I'll show you.

(MR BROWN gives his son the box of matches. JOHN lights a match and walks into the cave.)

JOHN	Can you see the holes above my head?
MRS BROWN	Be careful, John. Don't fall.

(JOHN puts his foot in a hole. It is full of water. He drops the matches and the cave is dark again.)

MRS BROWN	Now we're in the dark again.
MR BROWN	Have you got the matches, John?
JOHN	No, I've dropped them in the water.

MR BROWN	Then we'll have to leave.
MRS BROWN	Good. I don't like this place.

(MRS BROWN and MARY leave the cave. MR BROWN and JOHN follow. They stand outside.)

MR BROWN	Ah! It's nice to be outside again.
MRS BROWN	It's four o'clock. We should get back.
MARY	Oh look, the sea's coming in.
MR BROWN	Yes, it's come in a long way, hasn't it?
JOHN	It will soon reach the cave.
MARY	*(Pointing to the cliffs)* It's very near the cliffs.
MRS BROWN	Oh no! What about Granny? We left her on the beach. Perhaps she's fallen asleep. We should hurry back.
MR BROWN	I'm sure she's all right.
JOHN	I'll run back. Let's go, Mary.

(The children run off. MR and MRS BROWN follow them quickly.)

SCENE 3

(The place near the cliffs. JOHN and MARY arrive first.)

JOHN	Granny's not here.
MARY	Her chair's gone, too.
JOHN	*(Calling to his parents)* We can't see her, Dad.

(MR BROWN reaches the place. MRS BROWN follows him.)

MR BROWN	What's happened? Isn't she here?
MARY	We can't see her.

JOHN	*(Pointing)* She was there.
MARY	The sea's come in and covered that part of the beach.
MRS BROWN	We've lost her! *(She begins to cry.)*
MR BROWN	I can't believe it. The water isn't very deep.
MRS BROWN	*(Still crying)* But she couldn't swim!
JOHN	Look, there's her book. In the sea!
MARY	And her umbrella!
MR BROWN	But where's her chair? I can't see it.
MRS BROWN	It's at the bottom of the sea. With Granny on it. I've killed her! She wanted to sit near the cliffs, and I put her chair here.
MR BROWN	Don't cry, dear. It wasn't only you.
JOHN	The sea's coming in quickly. Shall I get the baskets, Dad?
MR BROWN	Yes, get the baskets. I'll look after your mother.

(JOHN and MARY go to the big rock near the cliff. Suddenly they both begin to laugh.)

MR BROWN	*(Angrily)* Why are you children laughing? This is serious, you know. We've lost your grandmother!
JOHN	Come and see, Dad.

(MR and MRS BROWN go to the rock. Then they too begin to laugh.)

MRS BROWN	It's Granny!
MR BROWN	And she's still asleep!
MARY	But how did she get here?
JOHN	And who carried her chair?

(GRANNY hears their voices and wakes up.)

GRANNY	Oh, you're back. Did you have a nice time? I've had a good sleep. What's the matter? Why are you all looking at me?
MARY	We couldn't find you, Granny.
JOHN	The sea's come in and we were worried.
GRANNY	*(Laughing)* Well, I was here all the time.
MRS BROWN	But how did you get here?
GRANNY	I walked here, of course.
MARY	But who carried your chair?
GRANNY	*I* did.
MRS BROWN	*(Angrily) You* did! At your age! You shouldn't do things like that.
GRANNY	Why not? I'm not a child, you know. Now, what about some tea?

A Bad Dream

SCENE 1

(GEORGE HILL is a bank manager, but he is not working today. It is Sunday afternoon. MR and MRS HILL have had lunch, made by ANNIE, their cook. They are now in their living room, drinking coffee.)

MR HILL	Ugh! This coffee's terrible. Why can't Annie make good coffee?
MRS HILL	I've tried to show her. She remembers for a few days, and then she forgets again. I'm afraid she isn't very clever.
MR HILL	You're right. She *isn't* very clever. And she's a bad cook, too. Lunch was terrible. I wanted to talk to you about it.
MRS HILL	About what?
MR HILL	Well, important customers come to our house for dinner and they get bad food. What will these people think of me? I'm their bank manager.
MRS HILL	If you're worried about it, *I'll* cook dinner for them next time. I won't let Annie into the kitchen.
MR HILL	No, you can't do that. You're my wife and you must meet these people. You can't spend your time in the kitchen.
MRS HILL	What's the answer, then?
MR HILL	It's easy. We must get a new cook.
MRS HILL	But Annie's been with us for a long time, George. Nearly twenty years. We can't do this to her. She isn't a young woman now. How will she find a new job?
MR HILL	I don't know, but she must go. Things are different now. I'm the manager of a big bank. We *must* have a good cook.

MRS HILL	George, what's happened to you? You've changed. You've become more selfish.
MR HILL	That's not true. I just want my customers to have the best, that's all. So Annie must go. Explain it to her. She'll understand. Give her three months. I'm sure she can find a new job in that time.
MRS HILL	It won't be easy.
MR HILL	Will you tell her?
MRS HILL	*(Sadly)* All right.
MR HILL	Good. Now, I feel quite tired. I think I'll have a little sleep.
MRS HILL	*(Getting up)* You stay here. I have something to do.

(Mrs Hill goes out of the room. Mr Hill puts his feet on a chair and closes his eyes. He is soon asleep.)

Scene 2

(Mr Hill is still asleep. There is a knock at the door.)

MR HILL	*(Waking up suddenly)* Who's there? Come in.

(Two men come into the room. They both work at the bank. Briggs is the assistant manager.)

BRIGGS	Good afternoon, sir. You're not busy, are you?
MR HILL	Briggs! And Winter! What is it? I was having a little sleep. Is it important?
BRIGGS	It's *very* important, sir.
MR HILL	*(Laughing)* The bank isn't on fire, is it?
BRIGGS	No, sir, but we had to see you.

MR HILL	Today? It's Sunday. I can't talk about work now. Come and see me in my office tomorrow.
WINTER	It can't wait, sir. We must talk to you today.
MR HILL	I don't understand. Well, sit down, both of you. *(The two men sit down.)* Now, what's the matter?
BRIGGS	It's not easy to begin, sir.
WINTER	Shall I tell him, Mr Briggs?
BRIGGS	No, I'll do it. I'm the assistant manager. Well, sir, we think you should resign.
MR HILL	*(Very surprised)* Resign? Leave the bank? What are you talking about? Is this a joke, Briggs?
BRIGGS	No, sir.
MR HILL	*(Sitting up in his chair)* Now wait a minute, please. It's Sunday afternoon. You come to my house and wake me up. Then you tell me . . . that I should resign?
WINTER	We're very sorry, sir. We know it's Sunday. But we had to tell you.
MR HILL	You can't speak to me like this. I'm your boss, or have you forgotten?
BRIGGS	We haven't forgotten, sir. But we're doing it for the bank.
WINTER	It will be a good thing for the bank, sir.
MR HILL	*(Standing up)* I've had enough! Go home, both of you. Take a holiday tomorrow. You both need a rest.
BRIGGS	We're all right, sir. We don't need a holiday.
WINTER	But we must have your answer today, sir. Will you resign?

MR HILL	*(Sitting down again)* It's like a bad dream! *Why* must I resign? What have I done? Tell me that.
BRIGGS	You aren't a good manager, sir.
MR HILL	*(Angrily)* That's not true. Thousands of people use our bank. Business is very good.
BRIGGS	Oh, we know *that*, sir. But *we* do all the work. They use our bank because *we* work hard.
WINTER	And you're not nice to the people in the bank. You're polite to the customers, but not to us. Nobody likes you!
MR HILL	Oh, I know they don't like me. They have to work hard, and they don't like that.
WINTER	But *you* don't work hard, sir.
MR HILL	Of course I do!
BRIGGS	You come to work late in the morning.
WINTER	And you often leave early.
BRIGGS	And you take two or three hours for lunch. We spend all day in the bank, but you're never there.
MR HILL	But I'm the manager. That's part of my job. I have to have lunch with important people. It's good for business.
BRIGGS	But that's not hard work, sir. It's fun for you. You enjoy good food.
MR HILL	I won't listen to this. I shall write to head office about you. Then *you'll* have to resign.
BRIGGS	We've already told them about you, sir.
WINTER	Yes, sir. We explained things to them and they agree with us.

MR HILL	What! You've written to head office? Without telling me!
BRIGGS	We had to do it, sir. We were only thinking of the bank.
WINTER	And they agree that you must resign.
MR HILL	But they can't do this to me! I've spent thirty years in the bank.
BRIGGS	Think of the bank, sir. It will be a happier place without you!
MR HILL	But what am I going to do? I'm not a young man. How can I find a new job?
WINTER	Oh, you'll find something, sir. A job in an office, perhaps.
BRIGGS	You don't have to leave immediately, sir. You can stay at the bank for two or three months. You'll be able to find a new job.
MR HILL	I'm not sure.
BRIGGS	But you promise to resign, don't you, sir?
MR HILL	Well, if head office agrees with you, I must.
WINTER	Thank you, sir.
BRIGGS	We're sorry about this, sir.

(BRIGGS and WINTER stand up.)

BRIGGS	You'll come to the office tomorrow, won't you, sir?
MR HILL	Er... yes, I'll be there.
WINTER	But please don't be late, sir.

(BRIGGS and WINTER say good afternoon and leave. MR HILL sits with his head in his hands. After a few minutes MRS HILL comes in. She is *wearing a coat and she has a bag in her hand.)*

MR HILL	*(Looking up)* Oh, it's you, dear. Briggs and Winter were here. They've just left.
MRS HILL	Yes, I saw them when they were going out.
MR HILL	They came to tell me something. It isn't very pleasant. *(After a minute)* I have to resign from the bank.
MRS HILL	Yes, I know.
MR HILL	*(Surprised)* You know already?
MRS HILL	Yes, they told me.
MR HILL	They couldn't wait! Did they tell you the reason, too?
MRS HILL	Yes, the people in the bank don't like you. I'm not surprised.
MR HILL	I've spent all my life in the bank and now I've lost my job. *(He notices that his wife is wearing a coat.)* Oh, are you going out? *(He sees the bag too.)* Where are you going?
MRS HILL	I need a holiday. I'm going to spend a few days with my sister.
MR HILL	At this time? But I need your help now.
MRS HILL	I can't help you. And I *must* have a holiday. I can't wait.
MR HILL	But you can have a holiday later. We'll go together.
MRS HILL	Where will you get the money for a holiday? You've lost your job. It won't be easy to find a new one. You're not a young man.
MR HILL	I've got three months. I'll find something.

MRS HILL	I hope you're right.
MR HILL	You're leaving me because I'm in trouble. When are you coming back?
MRS HILL	I have no idea. I'll write and tell you.
MR HILL	But who's going to look after me?
MRS HILL	There's Annie. Speak to her nicely and perhaps she'll stay. Well, goodbye, George. Write to me when you have a job.

(MRS HILL goes out of the room.)

MR HILL	*(To himself)* This is terrible! I've lost my job. Now my wife's gone, too!

(There is a knock at the door and ANNIE comes in.)

MR HILL	What is it, Annie? Do you want to leave, too?
ANNIE	Leave, sir? I came about the tea, sir. It's almost four o'clock. Shall I bring tea, sir?
MR HILL	So you don't want to leave. Are you sure?
ANNIE	No, of course not, sir. I'm very happy here.
MR HILL	I've lost my job. Did you know that?
ANNIE	Yes, sir, Mrs Hill told me.
MR HILL	And my wife has gone for a long holiday.
ANNIE	I know, sir. But she'll come back. I'll look after you while she's away.
MR HILL	I won't have much money. Perhaps I won't be able to pay you.
ANNIE	That doesn't matter, sir. I want to stay here, sir. It's my home.
MR HILL	Thank you, Annie.

28

ANNIE	Shall I bring tea now, sir?
MR HILL	Later, please. In about half an hour.
ANNIE	All right, sir.

(ANNIE goes out. MR HILL puts his feet on the chair again and closes his eyes.)

SCENE 3

(MRS HILL comes into the room. Her husband is still asleep.)

MRS HILL	George! It's almost half past four.
MR HILL	*(Waking up)* What's that? Half past four? Oh, it's you, dear.
MRS HILL	Yes, of course it's me.
MR HILL	You haven't gone to your sister's?
MRS HILL	What are you talking about? I haven't been out of the house. You've been asleep all afternoon.
MR HILL	Have I? Then I was dreaming. *(He remembers the dream.)* It wasn't a very pleasant dream.
MRS HILL	You must tell me about it. Shall we have tea now?
MR HILL	That's a good idea. I need a cup of tea!

(MRS HILL rings the bell for ANNIE.)

MR HILL	Have you spoken to Annie yet, dear?
MRS HILL	No, not yet. I've been busy. But I haven't forgotten. I'll tell her this evening.
MR HILL	I was thinking about it again. Perhaps we should keep her. She's been with us for a long time. She probably won't find another job.

MRS HILL	*I* told *you* that, dear!
MR HILL	I agree with you now. Of course she isn't a good cook, but she works hard.
MRS HILL	Yes, she works very hard.
MR HILL	Perhaps she needs help in the house. We can get someone.
MRS HILL	That's a nice idea. Annie will like that. But what about your dinners? Who will cook when your customers come?
MR HILL	Oh, the dinners aren't important. We won't ask people very often.
MRS HILL	I'm glad. I never liked those dinners. *(After a minute)* But, George, why have you changed suddenly? You're different now!
MR HILL	Am I? I'm glad you say that.
MRS HILL	Was it your dream? You must tell me about it.
MR HILL	No, I don't want to talk about it. But I won't forget it!

(ANNIE comes into the room.)

ANNIE	Shall I bring tea now, madam?

The Professor

PROFESSOR HUNTER

MISS GREEN

MR ROSE

MARY HUNTER

DR PITT

INSPECTOR HADLEY

SERGEANT BULL

SCENE 1

(MARY HUNTER is in her father's room, talking to MISS GREEN, the professor's secretary. It is a large, pleasant room, with a lot of books in it. There is a big desk near the window.)

MARY Dad's very excited this morning, Miss Green. He didn't want his breakfast. He only had a cup of coffee.

MISS GREEN Yes, of course he's excited. I'm excited, too. This is a very important day. He's ready to give his invention to the world. The papers are complete. I've just copied them.

MARY The men from the government will be here soon, won't they? They'll take the papers to London.

31

MISS GREEN	Yes. And then the professor will be famous! *(The telephone rings. MISS GREEN answers it.)* Hello? Yes, Miss Hunter's here. One minute, please. *(She gives the phone to MARY HUNTER.)* It's for you, dear. It's Dr Smith.
MARY	Good morning, Dr Smith . . . I'm very well, thank you . . . What's that? Freda's in hospital? Yes, of course I'll come. I'll be there in an hour. Goodbye. *(She puts the phone down.)*
MISS GREEN	What's the matter with your friend?
MARY	She's broken her leg and they've taken her to hospital. She wants to see me, so I must go. Oh dear! I wanted to stay here this morning. I wanted to look after Dad.
MISS GREEN	It's all right, Mary. I'll be here.

(The PROFESSOR comes into the room. He is an old man, and he cannot see well.)

PROFESSOR	I can't find my glasses. Have you seen them, Mary?
MISS GREEN	*(Going to the professor's desk)* Here they are, Professor. *(She gives the glasses to the PROFESSOR.)*
PROFESSOR	Ah, thank you, Miss Green. *(He puts on his glasses.)* I can't see anything without them. Now, what's the time? Hm, where's my watch? *(He looks for his watch in his pocket.)*
MARY	*(Laughing)* You're wearing it, Dad. I bought you a new one. Don't you remember?
PROFESSOR	*(Also laughing)* Yes, of course you did. I forgot. I forget a lot of things, don't I? But I can still do my work! That's the important thing.
MARY	Of course it is, Dad.

PROFESSOR	*(Looking at his watch)* It's almost ten o'clock. When are the men coming from London? They said 10.30, didn't they?
MISS GREEN	No, eleven.
PROFESSOR	Oh, I thought it was 10.30. It doesn't matter. I can look at my papers again.
MARY	Dr Smith phoned a few minutes ago.
PROFESSOR	Oh, what did he want?
MARY	My friend Freda's broken her leg and they've taken her to hospital. She wants to see me, so I have to leave now. I'm sorry I can't stay with you.
PROFESSOR	That's all right, Mary. Miss Green will look after me.
MARY	I must go, then. I'll be back at twelve. You can tell me about your morning then.
PROFESSOR	Goodbye, dear. Give my love to Freda.

(MARY kisses her father and goes out.)

PROFESSOR	Now... Ah yes, my papers. *(He goes to his desk and sits down.)*
MISS GREEN	Do you need me now, Professor?
PROFESSOR	Er, no thank you, Miss Green. I'll ring if I need you.

(MISS GREEN goes out of the room.)

PROFESSOR	Hm, these women! They think I can't look after myself. Sometimes I lose my glasses. Sometimes I forget about my watch. But they don't understand that those things aren't important. *(He begins to read his papers.)*

Scene 2

(Half an hour later. The PROFESSOR is still reading his papers. MISS GREEN comes into the room.)

MISS GREEN   *(Very excited)* They're here, Professor! They've arrived!

PROFESSOR   *(Looking up)* Who, Miss Green? What are you talking about?

MISS GREEN   The men from the government, of course.

PROFESSOR   *(Looking at his watch)* But it's only half past ten. They're half an hour early.

MISS GREEN   Shall I tell them to wait?

PROFESSOR   No, no, bring them in now.

(MISS GREEN goes to the door. Then she stops.)

MISS GREEN   Oh, they've shown me their cards, Professor. They're the right men.

PROFESSOR   Good. I don't want to give my invention to the wrong people!

(MISS GREEN goes to the door. She comes back with the two men.)

DR PITT   Good morning, Professor Hunter. My name's Pitt. Dr Pitt. And this is Mr Rose. He's my assistant. He's . . . looking after me. We don't want to lose your papers!

PROFESSOR   Lose my papers? No, of course not. Well, please sit down.

(MISS GREEN puts two chairs near the professor's desk and the two men sit down.)

MISS GREEN   Shall I bring some coffee?

DR PITT   No coffee for us, thank you. We can't stay long. We have to go back to London soon.

(MISS GREEN goes out.)

PROFESSOR So you've come for my papers. For my invention.

DR PITT That's right, Professor.

PROFESSOR I wanted to take the papers to you in London, but my daughter stopped me. It was too far for me, she said.

DR PITT That's no problem, Professor. We'll look after the papers for you.

PROFESSOR *(Looking round the room.)* Now, where did I put them?

(DR PITT is surprised. He looks at MR ROSE.)

MR ROSE There are some papers on your desk, Professor. Are they the ones?

PROFESSOR Oh, these? No, these are only some old papers. Ah, I remember now. I put the papers behind some books. *(He stands up.)*

DR PITT Behind your books? That's not a very good place for papers, is it?

PROFESSOR Yes it is. Nobody touches my books. *(He takes down some books. There are some papers behind them.)* Yes, here they are. *(He gives the papers to DR PITT.)* You know about my invention, don't you?

DR PITT Of course. We've often talked about it in the office. The government thinks your invention is very important. You'll be famous, Professor Hunter.

PROFESSOR I don't want to be famous. I only want to help people. So I'm *giving* my invention to the government. I don't want any money for it.

DR PITT The country will thank you for it, sir. *(He looks at his watch.)* I'm afraid we have to go now.

PROFESSOR   Well, look after the papers carefully.

(Dr Pitt puts the papers in his bag and stands up. Mr Rose stands up, too.)

DR PITT   Goodbye, Professor. We'll write to you.

PROFESSOR   Goodbye. *(He stands up.)*

(The two men go out. The Professor sits down at his desk again and laughs.)

PROFESSOR   Well, that was fun! Now we'll see what happens.

Scene 3

(It is about eleven o'clock. The Professor is still looking at the papers on his desk. Miss Green runs into the room.)

MISS GREEN   Professor! Those two men! Have they left?

PROFESSOR   *(Looking up)* Yes, of course they've left, Miss Green. They've taken the papers and they've gone back to London.

MISS GREEN   Oh, that's terrible!

PROFESSOR   *What's* terrible? What are you talking about?

MISS GREEN   *(Beginning to cry)* They were the wrong men, Professor!

PROFESSOR   I don't understand. You looked at their cards, didn't you?

MISS GREEN   Yes, but they stole those cards.

PROFESSOR   How do you know?

MISS GREEN   The police telephoned. The right men were coming from London. These men stopped the car. They locked the men in an empty house and stole all their papers. And now they've stolen your invention. What are we going to do?

(At that minute the doorbell rings.)

PROFESSOR   Go and open the door, Miss Green. It's probably the police.

(MISS GREEN goes out of the room. She comes back with two police officers.)

INSPECTOR   I'm Inspector Hadley, sir. And this is Sergeant Bull.

PROFESSOR   Please sit down.

(The two policemen sit down. INSPECTOR HADLEY puts his hat on the professor's desk.)

INSPECTOR   So those men have taken your papers. Your secretary's told us. But if you describe the men, Professor, we'll try to catch them.

PROFESSOR   It isn't necessary, Inspector.

INSPECTOR   Not necessary? I don't understand, sir. These men have stolen your invention, haven't they?

PROFESSOR   Oh, the papers aren't very important.

MISS GREEN   What are you saying, Professor? You've worked hard. You wanted to give your invention to the country. Now these men will sell it and make money.

PROFESSOR   Yes, I worked hard. That's true. But those two men won't sell my invention.

INSPECTOR   Why not?

PROFESSOR   Because I didn't give it to them!

MISS GREEN   Oh!

PROFESSOR	I'll explain. When I saw the men, I didn't like the look of them. You saw their cards, Miss Green, but I had to be sure. I couldn't give my invention to the wrong men, could I?
INSPECTOR	So what did you do?
PROFESSOR	Well, only one or two very important people know about my invention. When I asked Dr Pitt about it, he knew all about it. I thought that was strange.
INSPECTOR	What happened next?
PROFESSOR	I gave Dr Pitt some *old* papers. He read them and he accepted them. So he *didn't* know about my invention. I knew he wasn't the right man.
INSPECTOR	So you've still got the papers?
PROFESSOR	Yes, they're on my desk. They were there all the time.
INSPECTOR	But we must try to catch those men, Professor. Can you describe them to us?
PROFESSOR	*(He thinks.)* Dr Pitt was short and fat. And he had no hair.
MISS GREEN	No, Professor. That was Mr Rose. Dr Pitt was tall and thin.
PROFESSOR	Are you sure? Well, perhaps you're right. I can't remember things like that.
INSPECTOR	*(Standing up)* Don't worry, Professor. Miss Green will describe the men for us.

(The police sergeant stands up too. They go to the door.)

PROFESSOR	You've forgotten your hat, Inspector! *(He gives the hat to the INSPECTOR.)* Oh, Miss Green. I think *I'll* go to London this time. I'll take the papers with me. Telephone London. Say that I'll come on Monday.

MISS GREEN   All right, Professor.

(MISS GREEN and the two policemen go out.)

PROFESSOR   *(To himself)* Now for some work! Hm, where did I put my glasses?

ACTIVITIES

'Listen to the Boy!'

Before you read

1 What do you know about plays? Do you go to the theatre? Do you watch plays on TV? Do you act in plays? Discuss these questions and then read the Introduction and find out about these plays.

2 Look at the Word List at the back of the book. Find new words in your dictionary. Then complete these sentences with the words in *italics*.

cave scene cliff inspector head office sergeant
greengrocer's character manager smuggler granny

a The .... phoned me from ....

b My .... still buys all her vegetables at the local ....

c Two policemen arrived: an .... and a ....

d Hamlet is an interesting .... He dies in the last ....

e The .... hid the cigarettes in a .... at the bottom of the ....

3 Imagine that another customer pushes in front of you in a shop. How do you feel? What do you say to them?

While you read

4 What happens first? What happens next? Write the numbers 1–7.

a Mr Smith gives Mrs Ball some potatoes. .....

b Mr Smith speaks to Mrs Ball. .....

c Johnny tells a story. .....

d Mr Smith leaves the shop. .....

e A small boy runs into the shop. .....

f Johnny tells Mrs Wood his age. .....

g Mrs Ball asks for some potatoes. .....

5 Choose the correct word or words.

  a The first customer is *Miss White / Mrs Ball*.

  b She wants to buy some *apples / potatoes*.

  c *Miss White / Mrs Wood* decides to speak to Mrs Bell.

  d Miss White wants *greener / sweeter* apples.

  e The apples are stolen from Mr Smith's *car / shop*.

6 Work with another student. Act out this conversation.

  Student A: You are Johnny. Tell your mother what happened at the greengrocer's.

  Student B: You are Johnny's mother. Ask questions.

'The Right Person'

Before you read

7 Discuss this question. You have an empty room and you want to let it. These people are interested: a young man; a young woman with a cat; an old man with a dog, and an old woman. Which one do you want to let it to?

While you read

8 Are these sentences right (✓) or wrong (✗)?

The young man thinks . . .

  a the room is too big.

  b the furniture is too old.   .....

  c the bed is too soft.   .....

  d seventy pounds is too much.   .....

Mrs Stone tells the old man that:

  e the room is a long way from town.   .....

  f she and her husband are noisy.   .....

  g the room is warm in winter.   .....

  h the bed is soft.   .....

After you read

9 Find the correct endings, below, to these sentences.

  a Mrs Stone wants to let the room because ...

  b The young man doesn't like the furniture because ...

c The young man isn't interested in views because …

d The young man doesn't want breakfast because …

e Mrs Stone doesn't want an old man in the room because …

f The old man doesn't need buses because …

g Mr Stone gets pictures from the garage because …

h The picture is worth quite a lot of money because …

1) … he wants to cover the hole in the wall.

2) … people like John Holland's pictures.

3) … he enjoys walking.

4) … she doesn't want to look after him.

5) … she wants something to do.

6) … he is out all day.

7) … he gets up late.

8) … it is very old.

10 What do they say? Choose the correct words.

    a 'It's *little / a little* heavy.'

    b 'I get *bored / boring* at home all day.'

    c 'You can see a *far / long* way.'

    d 'He spoke very *nice / nicely*.'

    e 'I hope nobody *sees / doesn't see* the hole.'

    f 'Oh, that *isn't / doesn't* matter.'

'An Afternoon on the Beach'

Before you read

11 Discuss these questions. What is your favourite type of holiday? Do you like beach holidays? Why (not)?

While you read

12 Circle the correct word or words in *italics*.

    a John places Granny's chair *in / out of* the sun.

    b Granny wants a drink at *three / four* o'clock.

    c *Three / Four* of the Browns go to the cave.

    d Granny carries her chair to the *cliffs / sea*.

    e Granny's book is *in the sea / on her chair*.

    f *Mr Brown / John* finds Granny.

    g At the end, Granny wants some *sleep / tea*.

After you read

13 Who is speaking? What are they talking about?

    a 'Put them out of the sun.'

    b 'It's about two kilometres from here.'

    c 'Did they live here?'

    d 'No, I've dropped them in the water.'

    e 'Yes, it's come in a long way, hasn't it?'

    f 'It's at the bottom of the sea.'

14 Answer these questions.

    a Why doesn't Mrs Brown stay with Granny?

    b Why does Granny move her chair?

    c Why do John and Mary run back from the cave?

    d Why can't they find Granny?

'A Bad Dream'

Before you read

15 Look at the three people in the pictures on page 21. What do you think the job of the woman in the second picture is?

While you read

16 Who or what are these people talking about?

    a 'What will **these people** think of me?' ....

    b '**She** isn't a young woman now.' ....

    c '**It** will be a good thing for the bank, sir.' ....

    d '**They** have to work hard, and **they** don't like that.' ....

    e '**It** will be a happier place without you.' ....

    f 'It won't be easy to find a new **one**.' ....

    g '**It**'s my home.' ....

    h 'I don't want to talk about **it**. But I won't forget **it**!' ....

17 Work with another student. Act out this conversation from Mr Hill's dream.

> *Student A*: You are Mr Hill. You don't want to lose your job at the bank. Phone your boss at head office and ask him/her to think again.
>
> *Student B*: You work at head office and you have spoken to Mr Briggs. Mr Hill has to lose his job. Explain why.

'The Professor'

Before you read

18 Professor Hunter is an inventor. Discuss your favourite modern invention. Do you have one of these? Why do you like it?

While you read

19 Write the names. Who:

a copies the professor's papers for him?	....
b goes to visit someone in hospital?	....
c can't find his glasses or his watch?	....
d arrive early?	....
e is in a hurry?	....
f are locked in an empty house?	....
g asks the professor questions?	....
h has the important papers?	....

After you read

20 Answer these questions.

  a Why is the professor excited early in the morning?
  b Why can't Mary stay with her father?
  c What does the professor sometimes lose?
  d Does he think this is important?
  e Why didn't the professor take the papers to London?
  f Why is he giving his invention to the government?
  g Why can't the two men sell the professor's invention?
  h Why can't the professor describe the two men?

Writing

21 At the end of the play ('Listen to the Boy!'). Johnny goes home to his mother. He tells her what happened in the shop. Write their conversation.

22 The old man ('The Right Person') telephones a friend at the museum and describes the John Holland picture. His friend is very interested and asks questions. Write their conversation.

23 You are going to study at a college for six months. Write to the housing officer. Describe the room that you want. Can he/she help?

24 You are a tourist guide. You are going to take some tourists to the cave ('An Afternoon on the Beach'). You want to tell them about the smugglers and about activities that happened in the cave. Write down what you are going to say.

25 You are George Hill ('A Bad Dream'). After your dream, you decide to be a better manager. Write a letter to Mr Briggs about the changes that you will make at the bank.

26 Write a police description of the two men who tried to steal the professor's invention ('The Professor'). Use your imagination!

27 After he leaves Professor Hunter's house, Inspector Hadley follows the two men. After some time, he catches them. Write a newspaper report of this.

28 Which play did you enjoy most? Why did you like it? Was it because of the characters, the story or both? Write your ideas.

WORD LIST

act (n) one of the main parts of a play

basket (n) a strong bag that you carry things in. Baskets are often made from thin pieces of wood, plastic or metal.

cave (n) a large natural hole in the side of a rock or under the ground

character (n) a person in a play, book or film

cliff (n) a high, steep rock along the coast

doorbell (n) something on a front door that you press. When you press it, it makes a ringing sound inside the building.

greengrocer's (n) a shop that sells fruit and vegetables

granny (n) a name that you call your grandmother

head office (n) the main office that is the most important building for a company

inspector (n) a police officer

invention (n) an idea for something new; something that is made for the first time

let (v) to give someone the use of a room, flat or house for money

manager (n) the most important person in a bank, shop or team of people in an office

museum (n) a building where visitors can see important things from – for example – history or science

professor (n) the teacher with the highest position at a university in his or her subject area

resign (v) to tell your employer officially that you are going to leave your job

scene (n) a short part of a play or film. The action in a scene all happens in one place.

sergeant (n) a police officer with a lower position than an inspector

smuggler (n) someone who takes things unlawfully from one place to another place (from one country to another country, for example)

worth (adj) the amount that something can be sold for

Better learning
comes from fun.

Pearson English **Readers**

There are plenty of Pearson English Readers to choose from
- world classics, film and television adaptations, short stories, thrillers,
modern-day crime and adventure, biographies, American classics,
non-fiction, plays ... and more to come.

For a complete list of all Pearson English Readers titles, please contact
your local Pearson Education office or visit the website.

pearsonenglishreaders.com

LONGMAN
Dictionaries

Express yourself with confidence

Longman has led the way in ELT dictionaries since 1935. We constantly talk to students and teachers around the world to find out what they need from a learners' dictionary.

Why choose a Longman dictionary?

EASY TO UNDERSTAND

Longman invented the Defining Vocabulary - 2000 of the most common words which are used to write the definitions in our dictionaries. So Longman definitions are always clear and easy to understand.

REAL, NATURAL ENGLISH

All Longman dictionaries contain natural examples taken from real-life that help explain the meaning of a word and show you how to use it in context.

AVOID COMMON MISTAKES

Longman dictionaries are written specially for learners, and we make sure that you get all the help you need to avoid common mistakes. We analyse typical learners' mistakes and include notes on how to avoid them.

DIGITAL INNOVATION

Longman dictionaries are also available online at:
www.longmandictionaries.com or **www.longmandictionariesusa.com**

These are premier dictionary websites that allow you to access the best of Longman Learners' dictionaries, whatever you do, wherever you are. They offer a wealth of additional resources for teachers and students in the Teacher's Corner and the Study Centre.

Notes: